The Great Gatsby

(Gen Z Edition)

A Parody by Gwyneth Okerstrom

© Copyright Disclaimer

This work, *The Great Gatsby: Gen Z Edition*, is a transformative parody of the original novel *The Great Gatsby* by F. Scott Fitzgerald. It is intended for humorous purposes only.

This parody is protected under Section 107 of the Copyright Act of 1976, which allows for fair use for purposes such as criticism, comment, parody, and education. All characters and events are fictionalized reinterpretations and do not represent real individuals.

This is not a commercial reproduction or replacement for the original work, but rather a chaotic, unhinged, Gen Z-coded love letter to one of America's great literary tragedies — now with more slang, simping, and emotional instability.

No copyright infringement is intended. All rights to the original *The Great Gatsby* remain with the estate of F. Scott Fitzgerald and its publishers.

Table of Contents

Chapter 1: Vibe Check in West Egg.. 3
Chapter 2: Welcome to DepressionLand™......................... 11
Chapter 3: Clout Chasing w/ the Ghost of a Legend....... 20
Chapter 4: Trauma Dumping in a Rolls-Royce................... 28
Chapter 5: The Soft Launch of a Delulu Romance............ 35
Chapter 6: Who TF Is Gatsby?... 44
Chapter 7: Gaslight, Gatekeep, Gatsby................................ 52
Chapter 8: Ghosted by the Dream Girl................................ 61
Chapter 9: No One Came to the Funeral............................. 68
Author's Note.. 74

Chapter 1

Vibe Check in West Egg

When i was a young, goated and based little lad, my dad gave me a piece of advice that was basically S-Tier free therapy: "Whenever you feel like judging someone, remember: they might no cap just be doing their best with absolute garbage, so check your privilege." Which is deep. But also a little fake, because the man was *constantly* reading people.

Anyway, I still took that personally and became *so* nonjudgmental that I basically turned into a human sponge for everyone else's bad life decisions ●. People trauma dump on me at brunch, in cabs, at work, during birthday parties that aren't mine—

I listen. I nod. I absorb.

I am the group chat therapist.

👋 Hi, I'm **Nick Carraway**, and this is the story of how I became emotionally entangled with the most ✨aesthetic ✨ man alive: **Jay Gatsby.**

First, some backstory:

I'm from the Midwest — aka the beige part of America where ambition goes to take naps. My family is wealthy, but not like "diamond bathtub" wealthy — more like "we judge people who are." They sent me to Yale because legacy, and after graduating with a degree in Vibes & Polite Disillusionment™, I fought in the war.

🪖 The Great War, not the "my ex blocked me" war.

After the war, I tried living at home again, but honestly? The vibe was off. So I moved East to be a **bond guy**, which is code for "man who works in finance and knows literally nothing." I landed in **West Egg**, which sounds like a brunch order but is actually the part of Long Island where all the new money weirdos live.

Now, when I say "I rented a house," I mean I found the one crusty little cottage wedged between two Gatsbycore mansions like a sad eyebrow between two fierce brows.

To my right?
Gatsby's castle.
No joke — the man lives in a full-blown marble-wrapped Pinterest dream. Library. Pool. Tower. Lawn so sharp it could cut your feelings.

To my left, across the bay?

East Egg, where the old money lives.

People in East Egg have **Trust Fund energy**. Their families have been rich since the invention of shame. And right there on the edge is a mansion that belongs to my cousin: **Daisy Buchanan**.

Now Daisy is like... imagine if soft lighting and silk scarves became a person. She speaks in lowercase cursive. Her voice is so sweet and floaty it makes people confess things they didn't even know they were hiding. But don't let the sparkle fool you — she's mastered the art of sounding happy while being 90% existential crisis.

She's married to **Tom Buchanan**, who is a **walking bicep with entitlement issues**.

Tom is built like he was invented by toxic masculinity and gifted a polo shirt at birth. He's old money, dumb confident, and throws words like "civilization" and "white supremacy" around as if they're cocktail peanuts. 🚩🚩🚩

Anyway, Daisy invites me to dinner with her and Tom.
Their house? Marble everything. Plants arranged like they're paid actors. Breeze that smells like generational wealth and denial.

Also present: **Jordan Baker**, professional golf girl and recreational heartbreaker. Jordan looks like she's perpetually bored and vaguely judging everyone. She's got that dry, dry wit that makes you wonder if she's ever laughed for real.

Mid-dinner, Tom gets a mysterious call.
Daisy follows him out of the room.
Jordan leans over to me and drops the tea:

"That's his side chick. Lives in the city. The drama is *severe*."

When Daisy returns, she's trying way too hard to act unbothered.
She talks about her daughter (who is apparently real) and says something so tragic it knocks the wind out of me:

"I hope she'll be a beautiful little fool. That's the best thing a girl can be in this world."

💔 Excuse me ma'am??? That line alone deserves a therapy group and a feminist rewrite.

Later, after too much food and awkward silences, we all float out onto the porch where everyone pretends to be fulfilled. I go home confused, slightly tipsy, and thinking I've just witnessed something way deeper than dinner.

Back at my cottage, I see a figure standing at the end of Gatsby's dock.

👀 He's just standing there, arms out, reaching toward a tiny green light blinking across the bay — the one at the end of Daisy's dock.

He's not moving. Not speaking. Just... reaching. Like he's trying to touch a dream.

And in that moment, I realize:
This man is living in a fantasy he refuses to wake up from.

And me? I'm about to get emotionally drafted into someone else's love story.

Chapter 2

Welcome to DepressionLand™

Okay, so me and Tom are heading into the city, right? Classic dude's day out, I think. Maybe brunch, maybe light misogyny, maybe yelling at waiters. Very "rich men who peak in college" energy.

But nah.

Tom has other plans.

He turns to me, grinning like the final boss of red flags, and goes,

"We're making a lil stop first, Nick. Gotta see my girl ●."

My brain just *malfunctions*. Like, sir.

You're married.

You brought me to dinner with your *actual wife* last night.

And now you're doing this??

It's giving: "I cheat with confidence."

So we detour into this crusty stretch of road called the Valley of Ashes, which sounds poetic but is actually a gentrified wasteland powered by sadness.

It's like if a coal plant and a Spirit Halloween had a baby and then abandoned it emotionally.

Everything is gray. The sky? Gray. The buildings? Gray. The vibes? GRAY AF.

There's literally a giant billboard with two enormous

eyeballs looming over it all, like *Big Brother if he was an optometrist.*

 That's Dr. T. J. Eckleburg, watching silently like,

"●●● I saw that bad decision."

We stop at this garage, and that's where we meet George Wilson, who looks like he hasn't had a solid meal, a hug, or a single serotonin molecule in 10 years.

He's built like a soggy breadstick and speaks in lowercase.

Tom treats him like background furniture. No eye contact. Full alpha delusion. Just walks in like he owns the place (he doesn't — that's part of the problem).

And then. THEN.

From upstairs descends the ✨chaos goddess✨
herself:
Myrtle Wilson. Tom's side chick. George's actual wife.

She comes down those stairs like she's on the
RuPaul's Drag Race runway.
Red lips, attitude, heels that scream, "I know I'm the problem."
Like, it's giving:

"I'm married but I'm also vibing with your wallet."
And I respect that.

Tom gives her one nod — *just one* — and suddenly she's like

"BRB George, going to visit my sister 🫖"
and peaces out with us like she didn't just lie directly to her husband's Ashy Face.

Cut to: us in the city.

Tom brings us to his secret crash pad, aka Cheater HQ, which is decorated like a Crate & Barrel and a midlife crisis had a fight.
It smells like cigar smoke, broken promises, and knockoff Chanel No. 5.

Myrtle does a quick outfit change (because of course she packed a thirst trap look) and suddenly she's not Myrtle Wilson, Garage Wife™ anymore.

She's Myrtle 2.0: Downtown Diva Edition.

She invites over her chaotic little crew:

- Catherine, her sister, who looks like she's been kicked out of three astrology cults and now runs a chaotic crystals-and-cigarettes business.

- Mr. McKee, who claims to be a "photographer," but I'm 99% sure he just takes blurry photos of soup.

- Mrs. McKee, who exists.

Everyone's drinking like it's Prohibition (because it *is*), but Tom has connections and zero morals, so the liquor is flowing and the gossip is *scalding*.

Myrtle?
She's fully thriving in delulu land.
Saying things like:

"I told George we can't move because I'm too *refined* for the countryside."

Like ma'am. You're drinking bootleg gin in a cheating den.

She keeps name-dropping Tom like she's already soft-launched their relationship on IG. And then — the boldest move yet — she starts saying Daisy's name.
Over and over.
LOUD.

"Daisy. Daisy. DAAAAISY."

Tom tells her,

"Don't say her name."
But she keeps going.
Delulu has *entered the chat*.

So what does Tom do?

Does he leave?

Does he shut down the conversation?

No.

He decks her.

SMACK.

Out of *nowhere*, the man slaps her across the face and breaks her nose.

EVERYONE GOES SILENT.

It's giving:

🔔 "911 what's your emergency?"
🟢 "Yeah we're at Tom's house and it's a full crime scene now."

I'm just sitting there with my drink halfway to my mouth like:

"I thought we were doing brunch not domestic violence???"

The party dies.
The tension? STRATOSPHERIC.
Myrtle's bleeding, Tom's breathing heavy like he just hit the gym instead of a woman, and I'm contemplating jumping out the window.

Eventually, I black out.
Like, actually. Not metaphorically.

I wake up in the elevator or possibly in the void.
All I know is I get back to West Egg with a hangover and the haunting realization that my "chill Sunday" ended in blood, betrayal, and trauma™.

Chapter 3

Clout Chasing with the Ghost of a Legend

Let's talk about Gatsby.
The man.
The myth.
The guy whose parties have more lore than the MCU.

Every weekend, his mansion goes full ✨Euphoria Season 3✨.

No one knows how they got invited.
No one knows who invited them.
They just wake up in their little West Egg beds like

"It's Saturday. Time to black out in someone else's garden."

Gatsby's parties are so iconic that the streets start glowing. Champagne flows like LaCroix. There's music blasting, girls laughing, someone probably doing the Charleston on a roof. The entire mansion turns into a pre-Instagram thirst trap.

And here's the kicker:
He never shows up.
Or at least, no one can confirm it.
Some say he's CIA.
Some say he's a vampire.
One girl swore he once killed a man just for wearing the same tie.

So imagine my surprise when I get an actual, legit invite.

Delivered by a manservant in full tux, who's like,

"Mr. Gatsby cordially invites you to get turnt this Friday night."
And I'm like:
"Say less."

I get dressed up in my most *barely-passed-Yale-but-still-snatched* fit, pull up to the mansion, and immediately get hit in the face with vibes.

There's an orchestra playing like their lives depend on it.
There's enough food to feed Rhode Island.
And the fashion?
Serving full "I own 12 boas and zero self-control."

Inside, the aesthetic is chaotic elegance.
Every room is giving a different mood:

- One is Gatsby-core Versailles.

- One is 1920s rave cave.

- One is a library that smells like trauma and mahogany.

I link up with Jordan Baker, who's just... there.
Floating like a judgmental ghost in Gucci.
We start snooping around and trying to spot Gatsby like he's Bigfoot with bottle service.

We stumble into this library and meet Owl Eyes — this drunk little academic who's SHOOK that Gatsby's books are real.

Not hollow. Not fake. REAL.

He's sobbing like,

"He even cut the pages... he committed to the aesthetic!!"

Same, Owl Eyes. Same.

Eventually, Jordan and I are out on the patio sipping free champagne and gossiping when this guy slides up like:

"Hey old sport. Having fun?"

I'm like:

"Yeah, I mean—wait who are you?"

And he goes:

"Oh. I'm Gatsby."

EXCUSE ME??

No trumpets?
No glitter cannon?
No dramatic monologue??

Just, "I'm Gatsby," like he didn't just change the entire axis of this novel?

He's polite. Too polite. Like he's trying very hard to be *mysteriously charming* while also definitely hiding 12 crimes.

He talks in vibes. Not facts. Every sentence feels rehearsed.
He says he's from Oxford. Also San Francisco. Also "nowhere in particular."
Sir, what's your truth??

Before I can get more tea, he gets a *mysterious phone call* from Chicago (mob business?? MLM pitch???) and has to dip.

Later, he finds me again and invites me on a hydroplane ride (whatever that means), then disappears into the fog like a hot NPC.

Now, during the party, Gatsby's being a sweet little host:
Sending over butlers, checking that I have champagne, complimenting my Yale jawline.

He's obsessed with vibes and *control*. You can tell.

Everything's curated to look effortless — which means it took *so much effort*.

Jordan Baker pulls me aside with her usual

"I know something you don't ●"
 face and drops a secret:
 "Gatsby asked me to talk to you. He's planning something major. A plot twist. Stay tuned."

Girl, what???

The party starts to wind down around 2AM.
People are falling into fountains.
Cars are being driven by people who should not be driving.
One guest crashes his whip and stumbles out like,

"It's chill. The car doesn't need a wheel to vibe."

Iconic. Terrifying. Peak Gatsby party.

I stumble home full of mystery, glitter, and a vague sense that my whole life is about to get hijacked by someone else's dream.

Chapter 4

Trauma Dumping in a Rolls-Royce

So the morning after Gatsby's influencer mansion rave, I'm chilling on my porch nursing a hangover and some mild existential dread, when suddenly — vroom vroom —
a shiny car straight out of *Fast & the Flapperious* pulls up to my shack.

Out pops Gatsby like,

"Nick, old sport. Wanna go for a ride?"
And I'm like,
"Uhhh sure? Is this kidnapping? Is this love? Am I in a fanfiction?"

We hop into his car, which is less a vehicle and more a chariot of fragile masculinity — all chrome, horsepower, and big "I don't cry" energy.
We're zooming through the countryside at Mach 3, Gatsby swerving like he bought his license on Wish, when he hits me with:

"Let's get brunch later. I want you to meet someone... chill, normal guy... definitely not a criminal."

And then out of *nowhere* he decides it's time to trauma dump his entire backstory.

"I'm the son of wealthy, now-dead people in the Midwest. San Francisco, actually. Went to Oxford. Was awarded medals. I'm basically a war hero. And also rich. But not in a weird way. Just trust me, okay?"

He says all this with the energy of a man who definitely rehearsed it in the mirror every day for five years. He even whips out receipts — like a literal photo of him at Oxford and a war medal from Montenegro.

At this point I'm like:

"Is this a resume or are you trying to *gaslight me into loving you?*"

But hey, brunch is brunch.

We roll into Manhattan, and Gatsby takes me to this speakeasy disguised as a dentist's waiting room (because illegal activities require ✨aesthetic ✨).

Inside is this man with vibe violation written all over him.

Meet Meyer Wolfsheim.

He's old, sneaky-looking, and wearing human molars as cufflinks. Like literal TEETH.

It's giving "drinks warm milk and runs three illegal gambling rings before breakfast."

He's allegedly Gatsby's "business associate," which is 1920s code for "probably in the Mafia." Wolfsheim talks about fixing the 1919 World Series like it's a funny oopsie, and keeps saying Gatsby's the kind of man you can "really trust," which, fun fact, is what *liars always say.*

Gatsby is just sitting there smiling like a golden retriever who doesn't know it's a front for crime.

I try to excuse myself from this Mob & Mimosa moment, but Gatsby's like:

"WAIT — let's grab tea with Daisy sometime ●."

Oh yes.

Now we get to the real tea.

Turns out this whole *befriend Nick, invite to parties, show off my mansion, wear tight suits* thing?
It's not random.

It's Daisy.

It's always been Daisy.

Jordan Baker spills the whole latte:

"Gatsby and Daisy used to be a thing. Five years ago. War broke them up. She married Tom. But Gatsby? He's still down BAD. Like,
playlist-full-of-sad-boy-edits bad."

So what did Gatsby do?

- Moved across the bay.

- Bought a mansion next to her.

- Stared at the green light on her dock like it was a siren song.

- Threw weekly ragers hoping she'd show up.

- Befriended me *just* to get close enough to *orchestrate a surprise reunion like it's a prank channel.*

This man didn't just romanticize the past —
he straight-up built a personality around it.

I'm like,

"So he wants me to casually trap Daisy into a tea party where she walks into her ex's millionaire lair???"

Jordan just nods, sipping her drink like she didn't just drop a live grenade into my social calendar.

Chapter 5

The Soft Launch of a Delulu Romance

So Gatsby is spiraling.

I mean like, *real* spiraling.
We're talking

pacing-outside-my-house-in-the-middle-of-the-night-like-a-depressed-boyband-member energy.

He pulls up looking like a soggy heartbreak and is like:

"Nick, old sport… can you do me a teeny little favor and emotionally ambush Daisy for me?"

I blink.
This man wants me to set up a surprise reunion with

his ex, at my house, under the guise of "tea," like it's not actually a full-blown emotionally-charged soft launch of their situationship.

"Just invite her over... don't tell her I'll be there... I'll casually appear from behind a curtain like a simping magician."

And for some reason — maybe sleep deprivation, maybe peer pressure — I say yes.

Mistake #1.

Next morning, Gatsby goes absolutely feral with prep. Sends over a landscaper to mow my crusty lawn like we're prepping for *The Bachelor: Flapper Edition*. Then a truck pulls up with enough flowers to choke a Victorian poet.

My cottage now smells like anxiety and imported roses.

Gatsby shows up dressed like he's going to propose to Daisy *and* fight a duel *and* audition for a jazz band all at once.

He's sweating buckets, holding a bouquet, looking like he hasn't emotionally exhaled since 1917.

"Is the room okay? Is the lighting okay? Should I be visible right away or emerge slowly like a fog?"

I swear to god, he nearly flees the scene three times before Daisy even arrives.

Then Daisy shows up.

And it's instant panic.

She's dressed in soft pastels, glowing, floating like a perfume commercial with trust issues.
Gatsby sees her and instantly goes full emotional stroke.

This man FREEZES.
Just stands there like Windows XP trying to load a memory.

"H-hello…"

Silence.

No one breathes.
I'm holding tea like a hostage.
Daisy looks like she walked into the wrong Airbnb.
Gatsby looks like he might pee himself from emotional velocity.

So, naturally, I abandon ship.
 Fake a phone call and bounce, like:

"Y'all enjoy your trauma swirl. I'll be outside screaming into a bush."

When I come back?

The VIBE has mutated.

They're sitting together, whispering, crying, laughing — the emotional whiplash is giving me secondhand whiplash.
 Gatsby's glowing. Daisy's dabbing tears.
 I'm like,

"Did someone die or did you guys just emotionally reunite so hard it caused a weather shift?"

Gatsby invites us to his mansion because apparently, emotional closure requires a house tour.

We pull up and he's all:

"Welcome to the museum of my delulu coping mechanisms."

The man shows Daisy every hallway, chandelier, imported trinket and aggressively flexes like,

"This gold-plated clock? I bought it the year you got married because symbolism."

"These stairs? I cried on them once thinking about your voice."

"This flower arrangement? It means 'please regret your marriage.'"

We hit the bedroom and he opens his closet like:

"And now for the main event…"

He starts throwing shirts.
 Like, *launching* them.

Italian silk. English linen. Custom embroidery. Monogrammed sleeves. Shirts you have to be rich to even look at.
 He's flinging them at Daisy like they're Poké Balls and she's an emotionally unavailable Pikachu.

She starts crying.
 Like, full breakdown.

"They're just so beautiful 😭"

Girl. It's literally just a pile of designer laundry.
But also? Same.

Then we move to the balcony.

He points across the water and says it.

THE LINE.

"Look. See that green light? That's your dock. I've been staring at it... every night... for years."

Girl, RUN.

This man has been building an entire high-end fantasy novel in his head starring YOU — and now he's trying to manifest you into it like you're a limited-edition NFT.

And Daisy's just standing there like:

"Wow... romantic..."
 But also visibly recalculating all her life choices like a GPS losing signal.

Meanwhile, Gatsby is floating, fully convinced this is it.

She's here. They're back together. The universe is healed.

And I'm just watching from the corner like,

"Bestie, this is not a romance arc. This is a high-budget fanfic with ✨trauma glitter✨."

Chapter 6

Who TF Is Gatsby?

So, plot twist: Gatsby wasn't born in a velvet suit with jazz in his veins.

His real name?
James Gatz.
Like... sir. You sound like you work at an oil change shop, not a marble mansion.

He grew up in some dusty pocket of North Dakota where the biggest thrill was probably a new corn silo. His parents were like "just two chill peasants," but Gatsby woke up one day and decided:

"No thanks. I'm rebranding."

And rebrand he did.

He went full ✨DIY identity shift✨.
Grew a rich alter ego from scratch like he was cosplaying a Vanderbilt.
He started calling himself "Jay Gatsby" because "James Gatz" didn't sound like someone who'd own a gold bathtub.

At 17, he met this old rich yacht dude named Dan Cody, who basically looked like a walking cigar with money. Gatsby saved his life once — like, literally — and got taken in as a kind of emotional support butler.

They vibe for a while on yachts, drink too much, look mysterious. Gatsby sees the lifestyle and goes:

"Oh yeah. This? I want *all* of this."

Unfortunately, when Dan Cody unalived, Gatsby got nothing.

Dan's shady girlfriend finessed the bag and Gatsby got left on read by the will.
So, dreams? Shattered. Trauma? Unlocked. But ambition? Activated.

Cut back to the present.

Gatsby's throwing less parties now because he's fully tunnel-visioned on Daisy.
 He's like,

"The vibes aren't vibing unless she's here."
 So now the mansion is dead quiet, like an abandoned set from *The Real Housewives of Long Island*.

But don't worry — things get messy again fast.

Tom Buchanan starts getting sus.
He rolls up to Gatsby's mansion with Daisy, giving big "I'm fine, this is fine, I'm totally not insecure" energy.
He's pretending he doesn't care, but you can see the jealousy dripping out of his pores like Axe body spray.

Tom's basically like:

"So. You know this Gatsby guy? Weird how he has a mansion and charm and my wife's attention. Totally normal."

Gatsby invites them inside for a casual hang, and it's a whole circus.

Daisy's pretending she's not drooling over Gatsby, Gatsby's pretending he's not panicking every time she glances at Tom, and Tom is pretending he didn't Google "how to beat up a millionaire with a silk pocket square."

At some point Gatsby looks at Daisy like she's the sun and just goes:

"You didn't really love him, right?"
"Tell him you never loved him."

And Daisy's like:

"Wait. Uh... I mean... I *did* love him. But also I love you? So..."

Gatsby.exe has crashed.

This man has built his entire existence on the idea that Daisy's love was some sacred, undying, untouched little flower.

But now she's saying,

"Yeah, I loved you AND my actual husband. Sorry 💔"

Tom starts puffing up like a rabid lawn ornament, dragging Gatsby for being "new money" and calling his whole vibe fake.
 He even starts trying to expose Gatsby's business secrets like he's a villain in a courtroom drama.

"What do you even DO for money, huh? Is your name even Jay?? Are those cufflinks real gold or vibes???"

Daisy's watching them fight like she just realized this tea is *too hot to sip*.

The whole night ends with a weird, sweaty meltdown.

Tom insists Daisy and Gatsby ride back together like he's daring them to implode, which is... bold for someone who can't even keep his own mistress in check.

Back at the mansion, Gatsby's still in full denial mode.

He turns to me like:

"She's going to leave him. I just know it."

"We're going to go back to how things were. Like it was before. Like... five years ago."

And I'm just standing there, sipping my LaCroix, blinking slowly like:

"Sir... time is real. The past is not a Spotify playlist."

Chapter 7

Gaslight, Gatekeep, Gatsby

Okay. So Gatsby suddenly stops throwing parties. Dead quiet. Mansion locked down. Vibe: expired.

Why?

Because Daisy is finally hanging out with him in private, and he no longer needs to host ragers for strangers in hopes she'll walk in and say,

"Omg, is that my ex with a chandelier fetish?"

He fires his staff — like, the *entire* staff — and replaces them with shady dudes who look like they were grown in a lab to commit tax fraud. Apparently it's to keep things "discreet," but honestly the only thing discreet

here is Gatsby's grip on reality.

Then — it gets hot.
Like *heatwave from hell, thighs sticking to leather seats, brain melting out of ears* level hot.

It's the kind of heat that turns people into villains.

So naturally, Daisy calls me and says,

"Come to my house, we're doing luxury suffering today 🫖"

I roll up to Casa Daisy and the vibes are TOXIC.
 The AC is broken. Everyone's glistening with sweat and emotional instability.

Gatsby's there.

Tom's there.

Jordan's there.

Daisy is radiating main character energy and poor decision-making.

We all sit around pretending things are fine while *actively* suppressing the urge to scream.

Then Daisy makes the boldest move of the century and says to Gatsby,

"You always look so cool."

In a voice dripping with *please run away with me and never look back.*

Tom's like 👁️👄👁️

And the jealousy sets in IMMEDIATELY.

Man stands up like he's about to perform a monologue called
"Why Your Wife Should Not Flirt With Her Ex In Front Of You While You're Holding A Lemonade."

He suggests we all go to the city because clearly this house is not a big enough stage for his insecurities.

Now we split up into cars:

- Gatsby takes Daisy in his giant banana-yellow clown car.

- Tom, Jordan, and I pile into my sad little emotional support vehicle.

We get to the city and check into a random suite at the Plaza Hotel, which is approximately 1,000 degrees and smells like generational trauma.

Tom starts poking at Gatsby like a jealous frat bro at a college reunion:

"So Gatsby. Old sport, huh? That your thing? That your little catchphrase?"

"Tell me more about your... bootlegging and *definitely illegal* money?"

Gatsby's like

"Back off bro or I'll make you cry with my vibes and cologne."

Then it happens.

The Confrontation.

Gatsby turns to Daisy and is like:

"Tell him. Tell Tom you never loved him. Just say it. Say the line."

And Daisy's like:

"I—I loved you... but also... I guess I kind of loved him too???"

BOOM.
That's it.
Gatsby's soul leaves his body.
He built his whole dream life on the belief that Daisy's love was this pure, untouched, glowing little bubble and now she's out here admitting it's been shared??

He's shooketh.

Tom's gloating. Daisy's crying. Gatsby's imploding. I'm trying not to pass out from the combination of drama and heatstroke.

Eventually, the whole thing just collapses into silence.

Tom tells Daisy to ride back with Gatsby — like it's a *power move*, or a *final test*, or he just really wants to watch the world burn.

Then — chaos intensifies.

On the drive back through the Valley of Ashes, Myrtle — Tom's side chick — sees the yellow car.
She thinks it's Tom driving.
She runs into the road.

And gets hit.

Like, full-body yeeted.
Boom. Gone.
It's dark. It's tragic. It's *brutal out here.*

We pull up to the scene moments later and it's a whole horror movie.
Blood. Screaming. George Wilson (her husband) losing his entire will to exist.

Tom plays it *cool* — aka *absolute psychopath mode* — and is like:

"Yeah, it was Gatsby's car. Crazy, huh?"
He says this while holding Daisy like she's a Fabergé egg.

Meanwhile, back at my house, Gatsby is posted outside like a sad NPC waiting for a cutscene.

And he tells me the kicker:
Daisy was driving.

Yup.
Gatsby's out here *protecting her*.

Ready to take the fall for vehicular manslaughter. Because he loves her THAT much.

This man is simping so hard he's about to become a legal liability.

Chapter 8

Ghosted by the Dream Girl

So after the car crash of emotional and literal proportions, I wake up the next morning with a hangover made of guilt and spiritual humidity. Gatsby hasn't slept. At all.

He's still posted up like a golden retriever with abandonment issues, watching Daisy's mansion across the bay like she's gonna come outside and say:

"Sorry my husband's a villain and I ran someone over with your car. Let's kiss 💋"

Spoiler:
She doesn't.

Because Daisy is now officially back in Wife Mode™ and pretending the past 24 hours were just a weird little blip.

I go check on Gatsby and find him standing around in a full three-piece suit like he's expecting a surprise proposal, not emotional annihilation.

And what does he do?
Monologue time, baby.

He starts telling me — for the hundredth time — about the *summer of* 1917 when he met Daisy.
It's giving:

"We had one emotionally intense hookup and I've written 7 novels in my head about it since."

He says they were in love, sure.
But mostly, Gatsby was in love with the idea of

Daisy.

The glow. The money. The energy. The *aesthetic*.

She was his ✨main character origin point✨

and he's been doing a slow-mo TikTok spin about her ever since.

Meanwhile, George Wilson — Myrtle's sad husband — has officially lost his last brain cell.
He's walking around the Valley of Ashes like he's in an A24 film, talking to himself, and muttering about "the eyes of God" a.k.a. that dusty billboard with the creepy eyeballs on it.

Wilson is deep in his "vengeance arc."
He thinks the person who killed Myrtle must've been her lover.

Tom, ever the messy coward, told him Gatsby owns the yellow car.

So guess what Wilson does?

He goes hunting.

Back at Gatsby's house, Gatsby finally decides to use the pool for the first time all summer.
This man is trying to relax like he's not sitting in a boiling pot of trauma soup.
He's floating there, in his mansion pool, waiting for Daisy to call.
Because in his mind, this is still fixable.
She's just, like, busy? Having a moment? Reinstalling her emotions?

She's not calling.

But someone else shows up.

Wilson.

There's no confrontation. No slow build.
Wilson just shows up, pulls out a gun, and ends Gatsby's delulu dream in a single, horrible second.
No big speech.
No final words.
Just Gatsby face-down in the pool, the fantasy officially cancelled.

Then Wilson?
Turns the gun on himself.
One tragic man following another into the void.

Two lives — over.
And for what?
A dream. A green light. A lie.

Later, I'm at the mansion, phone in hand, *waiting* for someone — anyone — to care.

Nobody calls.
Nobody comes.
Daisy? Ghosted harder than a situationship after a second date.

Tom? Probably busy buying more shirts to cry into.

The phone rings.

I rush to answer.

It's not Daisy.

It's some random business guy, like:

"Hey, is Gatsby around? We had an appointment—"
Sir, the only thing Gatsby's attending now is his own funeral.

I look around the empty mansion.

No jazz. No guests. No Daisy.

Just silence.

And the body of a man who believed too hard, loved too deep, and ignored *literally every red flag* on the road to a dream that was never gonna happen.

Chapter 9

No One Came to the Funeral (Except Me and Some Birds)

Okay, so Gatsby is ✨officially deceased✨.
Shot in his own pool by a grief-stricken mechanic who got gaslit by Tom Buchanan.

And now?

Silence.

The house — once a glitter-drenched rave cave — is now giving haunted Airbnb.
No music. No parties. No one sliding into DMs to say,

"Sorry for your loss, bro 💔"

So I do what Gatsby literally *died* trying to do:
I wait for Daisy. I text. I call. I light a candle.
I refresh her Instagram like a clown.

She. Does. Not. Reply.

Sis straight-up vanishes with Tom like it's a 1920s witness protection program.
No funeral flowers. No "sorry for the vehicular homicide." Just ✌ and ✈.

So I start planning the funeral. Alone.

I call Gatsby's "friends" — all the party people, the clout-chasers, the name-droppers.
And every single one hits me with a variation of:

"Omg that's so sad... I'm just soooo busy this weekend 🫠"

"Tell him I said hey though 🕊"

Bestie...

he's DEAD.

Even Meyer Wolfsheim, Mr. Human-Teeth-Cufflinks himself, is like:

"Yeah I don't do funerals. Makes me feel icky."

The only person who shows up?

Gatsby's dad.

This sweet old man from North Dakota.
He pulls out a crumpled photo of Gatsby's mansion like it's a report card and says,

"He always dreamed big. Look at what my boy built."

And it's so sad.

Because Gatsby had all the glitter, all the luxury, all the fantasy

but in the end?

Only his dad and a man named Owl Eyes came to bury him.

The rest?

Too busy curating brunch aesthetics on their personal yachts.

The funeral is gray, soggy, and small.

And that's when it hits me:

Gatsby didn't die chasing Daisy.

He died chasing a version of her that never existed outside his imagination.

A vibe. A hope. A green light across the bay that

looked magical in the fog, but up close?
It was just... a porch light.

After that?

I'm *done*.

I call it. I pack up. I leave New York.
East Egg can choke.

I break things off with Jordan Baker too.
She's like:

"Wow, dramatic much?"
And I'm like:
"Yeah, it's called having morals and not ghosting dead people."

Then, the final moment.

I walk past Gatsby's mansion.

Empty now. Still.

No jazz. No lights. No dreams.

I stare across the bay at Daisy's house.

At that little green light blinking at the end of her dock.

The one Gatsby believed in.

The one he let define him.

The one he unalived for.

And I think:

We cringe on. Boats against the current.

Dragged back into the algorithm.

Chasing dreams we'll never catch,

Vibing with ghosts,

Crying over linen shirts.

Author's Note

Thank you so much for reading *The Great Gatsby: Gen Z Edition*. This project began as a lighthearted idea — a way to reimagine a literary classic through the lens of modern language and humor. Somehow, it turned into a full book.

I hope it made you laugh, smile, or simply see this timeless story from a different perspective. It was written with genuine affection for the original, and if it brought you even a little joy, then I consider that a success.

Thanks again for joining me on this unexpected journey. It truly means a lot.

— Gwyneth Okerstrom

Printed in Great Britain
by Amazon